HOW TO DESIGN AN EFFECTIVE SYSTEM FOR DEVELOPING MANAGERS AND EXECUTIVES

D1315368

HOW TO DESIGN AN EFFECTIVE SYSTEM FOR DEVELOPING MANAGERS AND EXECUTIVES

Maxine A. Dalton
George P. Hollenbeck

Center for Creative Leadership
Greensboro, North Carolina

The Center for Creative Leadership is an international, nonprofit educational institution founded in 1970 to foster leadership and effective management for the good of society overall. As a part of this mission, it publishes books and reports that aim to contribute to a general process of inquiry and understanding in which ideas related to leadership are raised, exchanged, and evaluated. The ideas presented in its publications are those of the authors.

The Center thanks you for supporting its work through the purchase of this volume. If you have comments, suggestions, or questions about any Center publication, please contact Walter W. Tornow, Vice President, Research and Publication, at the address given below.

Center for Creative Leadership
Post Office Box 26300
Greensboro, North Carolina 27438-6300

CENTER FOR CREATIVE LEADERSHIP

CCL No. 158

Library of Congress Cataloging-in-Publication Data

Dalton, Maxine A.
    How to design an effective system for developing managers and executives /
Maxine A. Dalton, George P. Hollenbeck.
        p.   cm.
    Includes bibliographical references.
    ISBN 1-882197-24-0
    1. Executives—Training of. 2. Industrial management—Study and teaching.
I. Hollenbeck, George P. II. Title.
HD30.4.D355 1996
658.4'0712404—dc20   96-28862
                                                                         CIP

Table of Contents

Preface

For a number of years we at the Center for Creative Leadership have been conducting a program called "Tools for Developing Successful Executives." It teaches human resources professionals to design programs of development within their own organizations. The curriculum for this program represents an ongoing exchange of ideas and information between CCL's research and applications staff and the more than 1,000 human resources practitioners who have attended the course.

Often, after the program is over, participants ask for additional concrete information about implementation of the tools they have learned. This report is in response to those who have the information on paper or in their heads on how to design a development program but ask, "How do I actually *do* it?" It is not a fix-it guide for the remediation of employee performance problems, although much of our discussion addresses that issue. Our focus is on how to put in place programs of structured activities that will allow individuals to learn particular skills or acquire the frames of reference required for success as managers and executives, concentrating particularly on program design and the elements of individual development within a process.

Because our guide has been so much informed by participants in the Tools program, in a sense those individuals were our consultants in preparing this report. We thank them and acknowledge their substantial contribution; we hope that after using this report, you, too, will thank them for their wisdom.

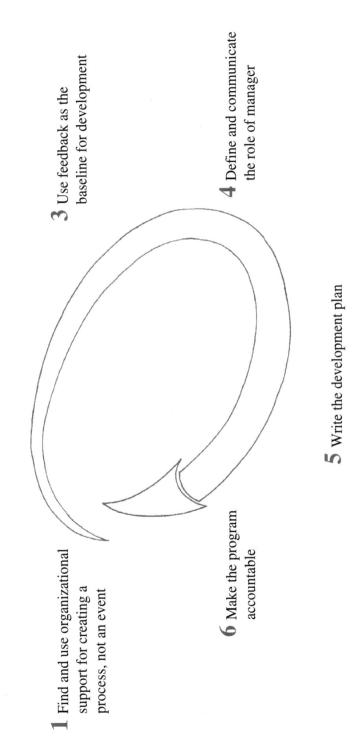

2 Define program purpose and behaviors

3 Use feedback as the baseline for development

4 Define and communicate the role of manager

1 Find and use organizational support for creating a process, not an event

6 Make the program accountable

5 Write the development plan

Model for Developmental Planning

Executive Guide
A Summary of the Basic Steps to Developmental Planning

STEP 1: Find and Use Organizational Support for Creating a Process, Not an Event

When initiating a program for development, recognize and respond to the catalyst for the program. Design a development process that may include a training event but is not, itself, the sum total of the program for development. Find a champion. Pilot your efforts. Solicit and use feedback. Move in a timely fashion. Take organizational readiness into account as you design the process. (See pages 3-7.)

STEP 2: Define the Program Purpose and the Behaviors to Be Developed

Program purpose should align with the business needs of the organization. Skills targeted for development should be appropriate to time frame, level, and program purpose. When managers need to acquire the basic skills required to coordinate people and resources to accomplish an organizational goal, the skills being developed will speak to the here and now of the manager's job. Identification of these skills requires a content-validation strategy or the adoption of an existing research-based model of managerial effectiveness.

The targeted skills for the development of future leaders need to be based on a predictive validity strategy, an approach that defines needed skills in light of anticipated business direction, and should reflect the best thinking of senior management about the conditions that will prevail at the time these managers will take on the responsibilities and accountability of executives. What needs to be learned will dictate how it is learned. (See pages 8-17.)

STEP 3: Use Feedback as the Baseline for Executive Development

Feedback is one of the events that make up the program of development. Our feedback guidelines are designed to increase the odds that you will succeed in generating energy and direction for change from the feedback element in your program. Our emphasis is on credibility. To be credible feedback must be meaningful, aimed at potential, confidential and anonymous, and timely. It can be provided from simple interviews or professionally developed instruments, each of which has its advantages and disadvantages. The effectiveness of any feedback process depends on the skill of the feedback-giver.

Although our goal with feedback is to provide direction and energy for change among participants, inevitably some will attempt more change than others. Those whose feedback is much different than their own self-evaluation are more likely to change. More change takes place where there is a supportive boss and a supportive organization. (See pages 17-22.)

STEP 4: Define and Communicate the Critical Role of the Manager

Managers are critical to the development process. They have a number of key roles that they must endorse, understand, and have the skills to carry out. These include: making development real, providing developmental experiences, providing support and feedback, and accessing organizational resources. Bringing the managers on board to their roles and the program is a critical task of the human resources professional. But the task does not stop when the program begins—managers require continuing support to fulfill their developmental roles. (See pages 22-24.)

STEP 5: Write the Development Plan

The elements of the process of writing a development plan provide a checklist for the program developer, but the process itself takes place as a whole. It can be simple or complex, brief or lengthy, committed to paper or largely in the head of the participant. The elements of the process (a goal, action steps and milestones, and standards) and the roles (executive, manager, and facilitator) must all be in place within an organizational context that supports development. We realize that development planning usually takes place without having all these elements in perfect harmony. At the same time, these elements have a major impact on the success of the development-planning effort and your success in making it happen. (See pages 24-34.)

STEP 6: Make the Program Accountable

Providing a regular stream of evaluation information is critical to maintaining the credibility and continuation of the development program. Two types of evaluation are needed: First, is the program being followed as laid out—are the development plans active? Second, are participants developing? Evaluation can be conducted at many levels, depending on the types of information needed and the resources available. The most important point is to feed from the beginning a regular stream of evaluation information back to the organization to demonstrate the value of the program. (See pages 34-36.)

Acknowledgments

The authors would like to thank the reviewers—CCL's Writers Advisory Group; Tanya Clemons, Georgia-Pacific; Tim Hall, Boston University; Mary Jane Knudson, Digital Equipment Corporation; and Ed Levine, University of South Florida—for their time, insights, and suggestions.

We would like to especially thank our editors at CCL—Martin Wilcox and Marcia Horowitz—for their consistent, knowledgeable, and thorough work on our behalf.

Introduction

At CCL we believe that development of managers and executives depends on a combination of ability, willingness to learn, and opportunity. Frequently, not much can be done about the first two—ability or willingness to learn; so helping the person develop must focus on opportunity—providing the opportunities to learn in a way that maximizes the odds that learning, growth, and development will take place.

This report offers a model for a process of development planning that provides such opportunities. It is based on the "Tools for Developing Successful Executives" program, and is meant to capture its lessons and put them in usable form.

The model has six steps (each covered in its own section):

1. Find and use organizational support for creating a process, not an event.
2. Define the purpose of the program and behaviors to be developed.
3. Provide feedback for target participants, giving them baseline information about their current skill level and showing them how they can improve or learn new skills.
4. Define and communicate the role of the manager in development and orient the manager to the program.
5. Help participants write and use a development plan.
6. Make the program accountable by defining the outcome measures that capture the program purpose and evaluate the program against those measures.

If you are new to the field of human resources development or at the beginning of your own design effort, we intend that the model be used sequentially and cumulatively. Each step leads to the next. The program designer has to consider the impact of each step on what has gone before and what will follow. For example, you will see that buy-in and support (Step 1) is built on accountability (Step 6). Accountability is built on clarity of program purpose (Step 2), and so forth.

If you are an experienced HR development practitioner or if you are trying to evaluate and improve an existing program, we offer the model as a checklist, a way to review each of your components to determine if the sense of purpose, implementation, and accountability flow in a logical way from the business need that is driving the program toward the outcomes that the business wants.

We suggest that you think of the six steps as you would instructions for building a model airplane. Lay out all of the pieces first. Make sure all of the parts are there. Read through the instructions before you start. Think about how the parts fit together.

Writing about development planning presents language problems. What do we call the target of our development efforts—the person whom we hope will develop? And what do we call that person, key in the development process, who used to be called your *manager,* or boss, or supervisor, but who may in the modern organization do very little traditional managing?

We have adopted a convention that we think will be clear. The person whose development we are planning we will call the *participant*—whether an engineer or salesperson, a manager with a formal hierarchy, or a team leader with limited traditional supervisory responsibility; or whether an executive somewhere on the rungs of the executive ladder—but not so high as to be the "boss of all bosses." The individual with administrative responsibility for the development of this participant we will call the *manager,* again recognizing that our usage may not reflect the complexities of the authority relationship in the modern organization, and that in using *manager* we may be referring to a person with no formal subordinates or with thousands.

We also want to alert you to our use of the word *program.* As will be clear in this report, we want to present development as a process and not as an event. Programs of development occur as a result of many interlocking steps and events over time, each building on what has gone before. Developmental programs may be punctuated by events, such as receiving feedback in a formal 360-degree-feedback activity, but that event is not the program. We will use the term *program* to refer to the entire process of development, and terms like *step, event,* or *activity* to refer to program components.

There is yet another caveat about the use of language. Throughout this report we refer to the human resources professional as the person who designs and conducts the development program. We know that there is a subgroup of professionals within the HR function called the human resources development (HRD) professional. However, not all HR professionals who practice development may hold that title if they are in smaller companies or perform a variety of HR functions. Therefore, we refer to the person who does the design and development as the HR professional.

Whatever words we use, we ask your translation to any form that will help you further the process of development planning in your organization.

STEP 1: Find and Use Organizational Support for Creating a Process, Not an Event

Finding support for creating a process of development involves helping the organization understand and thus commit to a program of development that acknowledges the reality of how adults learn, grow, and change over time. Adults learn what they need to know. This means that a program of development must be tied to business need and the day-to-day work of the organization. The HR professional must find support for building a program of development around these two basic requirements. As the following discussion illustrates, this is not as easy as it sounds.

Executive development programs abound in business and government today. The establishment of a program is often triggered by some untoward organization event: Attitude survey results show that the troops are unhappy with development opportunities; the "good" people are leaving; when an opening comes up, there is nobody in the pipeline, so you have to go outside; there is a high failure rate among high-potentials; perhaps the direction of the business is changing and executives are needed who have a "new skill set"; or maybe there is simply an amorphous wish to "do something for our people."

Whatever the catalyst, when the HR professional receives the call to design a development program, the client organization often has a preconceived idea of what it wants: "Give us a training program that will solve these problems." This is a seductive invitation—most HR professionals can design a training class that will hold people's attention, receive high ratings, and not interfere too much with business as usual. Unfortunately, it is not likely that any single class will cause much change in the behavior of the participants.

Training programs may deliver content knowledge. They may increase self-awareness. They may unfreeze attitudes. They may model or describe a particular process or point of view. They may provide a wonderful opportunity to meet colleagues in the field. But the training program is, by itself, unlikely to provide much that is significant enough to be cited by executives as critically important in their growth or as having had much impact on business results (McCall, Lombardo, & Morrison, 1988).

A central theme of CCL research, replicated time and again, is that development takes place on the job far more often than in the classroom. And although development happens whether we plan it or not, the good news from our research is that we can increase the odds that it will happen more quickly and in the needed directions.

To design an integrative process rather than a singular event, job experiences must be built into the development program. We offer this, however, in the face of the fact that a training program is often the "tool of choice" for a number of attractive reasons: It can be handed over to the training department; it requires little disruption of the ebb and flow of daily work; it doesn't take much of the manager's or the executive's time; and it doesn't demand that either of them do much that they are not already well-equipped to do. We believe, however, that doing development planning properly means that it is necessary to integrate experience into the development program.

Where does the energy to support designing a process come from? First, it comes from tapping into the natural flow that drives the business toward results. Our key principle here is this: You, as an HR professional, can never overestimate how much the business manager is focused on getting results. Tie development into that central purpose and the demands for sound development programs will exceed your expectations. Our experiences have identified a number of approaches that work.

Seek a Developmentally Friendly Manager as Your Partner

Effective development programs are interventions, not events, so even though a program may in your mind be tied to results of unquestionable value, starting with a developmentally friendly manager makes your task easier. It will allow for building a pilot program, demonstrating success to the rest of the organization, and breaking free of the short-term, one-shot training model. Developmentally friendly managers come in all shapes and sizes, ages, and functions, and usually they are well-known within the organization: High-potentials want to work with them; they export top-notch people to other areas; they believe that people produce results. For example:

> One HR professional told us that he was fortunate enough to be able to introduce and pilot his program with the CEO and the CEO's direct reports. To demonstrate his support for development, the CEO wrote up his reflections about the experience in the company newsletter, even outlining his own developmental goals and presenting his strategies for working on these goals. He modeled for the organization that learning is a valued and even requisite activity for successful people in the organization.

> Another HR professional piloted her program within HR. Because the director of HR believed that development was critical to the organiza-

tion, he was supportive of the initiative within his group. The members of the group not only personally benefited from the intervention, but they had the skills to give the program designer some useful feedback about the program itself before it was exposed to a larger and more critical part of the organization.

Educate Key Decision-makers

Another tactic to sell the program internally is to employ what has come to be known in our Tools program as the "key-events questions." Senior decision-makers in the organization are asked to respond to the following questions:

> When you think about your career, certain events or episodes probably stand out in your mind—things that led to a lasting change in you as a manager. Please identify a key event in your career, something that made a difference in the way you manage now. What happened? What did you learn from it? What were the challenges of the experience? How did you learn what you learned? What was going on in the environment that allowed you to learn?

As the group shares its answers, the facilitator takes the opportunity to point out that just as these executives have experienced major learning from the events of their careers, it is also possible to incorporate that understanding into a program of development that makes experience intentional and purposeful, fully integrated with the work of the organization. A part of CCL's initial research on how executives develop (McCall et al., 1988), these questions have remarkable impact. Almost all managers enjoy reviewing their personal key events. They are eager to talk to others about them, and they quickly see how important job experiences have been to their own development.

They will discover, like our research samples, the kinds of key experiences that truly develop. They will also find that their organizations are doing remarkably little to assure that executives have the opportunity to experience these key events for themselves. Their stories illustrate that development occurs within a variety of experiences, including challenging job assignments and work tasks, working with especially competent (or incompetent) other people, in targeted coursework, and even during hardships (McCall et al., 1988; McCauley, Ruderman, Ohlott, & Morrow, 1994; Wick & León, 1993).

As the HR professional, you can use the following exercise as illustration and example of how it is possible to structure and prescribe developmental activities; to move from the serendipitous to the intentional.

Here is how one company used the key-events questions to get the attention of its senior management:

> Because the president of the company was vaguely interested in establishing some sort of system of succession, the HR development specialist was able to get on the agenda of the quarterly meeting of the president and division heads for a two-hour presentation. Interestingly and coincidentally, each of the divisions was facing a very different set of business challenges. One was in retrenchment; one was in a growth mode introducing some exciting new products; and another was recovering from a downsizing experience two years past. In other words, each division required a different set of managerial and leadership skills and, therefore, provided individuals with the opportunity to learn and use those skills.
>
> There was no history of individuals moving across divisions. The HR specialist used the key-events exercise to get this fairly gruff and reticent group to talk about their own careers and how they had learned. He introduced the notion of intentional learning from experience, using the divisions as the classrooms, each with a different set of lessons to be learned. The exercise "took," and the HR specialist was asked to spend the remainder of the day with the group to discuss ways that such a system could be implemented. Because the key-events exercise reflected their own experience and the developmental strategy was integral to the business problems the group was facing, this group of managers decided that a program of development built on the experiences of the workplace was reasonable, practical, and desirable.

Pay Attention to Timeliness

Another guideline for gaining support is to strike while the iron is hot. HR professionals can sometimes spend so long on developing the program that by the time it is ready to go, the energy is lost or the organization has lost interest. Start small, if need be, and plan small wins along the way.

A commonly used approach is to benchmark—find out what other companies are doing and use that to capture interest. What GE or BellSouth or Pepsi is doing may or may not have anything to offer your company, but every company (and every CEO) has organizations with which they like to compare themselves. If these companies are doing a terrific job on development planning, take your senior management to see the process firsthand. And if they are not doing anything, here is your chance to steal a march on them, to move to another league.

The HR professional has to gather data—making the case with business results, not as an advocate for some "fuzzy-headed concern for people." In a *Wall Street Journal* interview (January 17, 1995), Mike Hammer is quoted, "The biggest lie told by most corporations, and they tell it proudly, is that people are our most important assets." Don't make the mistake of basing your case on the statement in the annual report—gather data, cases as well as numbers, where executive success or failure was the difference in business outcomes, both in your organization and without.

Employ Patience and Persistence

If you don't succeed at first, keep on trying. The time may not be right; the organizational attention may be on something else; the resources, however small, may not be there at the time. Our hope is that you will take solace in the fact that timing is everything, and it may just not be time.

Both organizational and individual readiness will be key factors dictating the scope and purpose of the process you design and the events you incorporate into the program. If you are clear about the limits that readiness places on what can reasonably be expected from the program, then even modest gains can be recognized as accomplishments.

Recently one of the authors received a call from someone who was in the Tools course two years ago. She said, "I finally got their attention. They are ready to go!" I asked her what made the difference. She told me their third external hire had just bitten the dust and the senior team decided it must start to develop internal talent. Buying talent was not working for them.

For further information, see:

Hall, D. T. (1986, Summer). Dilemmas in linking succession planning to individual executive learning. *Human Resources Management, 25*(2), 235-265.

STEP 2: Define the Program Purpose and the Behaviors to Be Developed

Step 2, defining program purpose, might sometimes be Step 1. The process we are outlining is a sequential interlocking process but is not lock-step. The sequencing of these two steps depends upon the clarity of the call. If you, as the HR professional, are approached with a vague request for a program, you most likely will have to build support before you can hone in on purpose. If purpose as defined in this section is clear at the beginning, then finding support may become Step 2.

Whatever the sequence, the HR professional plays a key role in clarifying the purpose of the program to be developed and assuring the tie-in to important organizational outcomes. Effort spent addressing the questions, Why do we need this? Who is it for? and What outcomes do we expect? has a positive impact in proportion to the time and cost expended. The graveyard of development-planning programs is filled with the skeletons of ill-defined ventures whose outcomes were not clearly laid out. Here is an example:

An HR specialist became intrigued with a particular feedback instrument. He was able to convince his boss that feedback would be helpful to people, and in the flush of good economic times launched a program where more than 500 individuals received feedback in a fifty-person, two-hour group setting over a six-month period. There was no thought given as to why feedback might be helpful to people or what the outcomes of this event might reasonably be. All of the time, energy, and dollars went into the administration of the logistics to deliver the feedback. Ten months later the managers in the organization were totally burned out by this event. Individuals who had been taken through this maelstrom of activity were angry, disappointed, or cynical about unmet expectations as to where the feedback might lead. A lot of money had been spent.

There was no follow-up to the feedback event and no obvious behavior change in those who had received the feedback, so when the inevitable economic downturn came the HR specialist lost his job. The event of feedback had become the end rather than a means to an end. This program had no stated purpose or measurement of impact.

Program Purpose

The organizational needs that are reflected in the purpose may be quite varied; for example, increasing employee satisfaction; establishing employee ownership for career direction; enhancing the skill level of managers at a particular level; developing leadership skills in a group of high-potentials to complement the strategic direction of the organization; or providing candid feedback to someone at the top perceived to be static, behind the times, or unaware of his or her impact. These are often the flip side of the "untoward events" described in Step 1 (poor morale, high turnover, and so forth). And the purpose may be multiple—programs can serve more than one master. The key is that up front the HR professional and senior management must understand what they are trying to do and why.

Our principle here is: The program purpose must reflect organizational need. Intended purpose not only defines the program content, it also defines the desired outcomes and therefore addresses evaluation and accountability issues at the beginning of the program, not as an afterthought at the end.

Need, purpose, outcome, and result are different statements of the same fact. Participant behaviors to be developed are the bridge between need/purpose and outcome/result. Here are two examples that illustrate the links:

The organizational need is to reduce the costs of turnover attributed to poor morale. The program purpose is to increase morale. The desired participant behavior to be developed is a more collaborative and team-based management style. The outcome is increased morale. The result is lower turnover and a reduction of expense associated with recruitment.

The organizational need is to have individuals ready to replace senior managers at retirement. The program purpose is to develop bench strength. The desired participant behaviors include complex cognitive and interpersonal skills. The outcome is a pool of potential executives with the requisite skills. The result is bench strength.

When a program is well thought out, need, purpose, outcome, and result are logical restatements of one another. Whatever specific outcome is sought, if the development-planning program is to be long lasting, the purpose and outcome must address the need and be integral to the business of the organization.

HR professionals are often urged to tie development to the strategy of the organization. This is often far easier said than done. The business strategy may not be readily available because it hasn't been articulated, at least not in a form the HR person can access. Or the link between the program, the expected outcomes, and the business strategy may require more knowledge of a complex business than the HR person may have.

In a recent paper, Seibert, Hall, and Kram (1995) have suggested an approach to partnering with the manager that recognizes these complexities as well as the changing nature of strategies. They point out that the HR professional will seldom have the in-depth knowledge of a complex business as does the unit manager. But the HR professional may be able to depend on the unit manager to know and articulate the business outcomes that will be most relevant for providing concurrent opportunities for development.

Each brings his or her expertise to the table. The unit manager knows where the business is going. The HR professional knows how to use that information to serve the purpose of development. Development is not separate from work but is an integral part of the work itself.

The area in our model between the need/purpose and the outcome/result is the critical HR professional contribution—building development programs that are likely to produce behaviors that will in turn result in the outcomes that will move the organization forward toward its goals. Understanding this chain of elements from business need through organizational results is essential to the design of the overall program. Here is an example of the importance of understanding this chain:

> An HR professional, an outside consultant, got the call one Monday morning—come up to the CEO's office to talk about a training program. As she listened to the CEO talk, it soon became clear that the company, an engineering construction division of a larger company, really had no strategy. The CEO could not specify what behaviors were needed because they had not thought through what they wanted to accomplish. The meeting became the first step in a process of defining where the business was going and what organization (jobs, units, and so forth) would be needed to support that direction. Working through the elements the executive team then determined what behaviors would be needed to effect success, and in turn what HR processes should support the new behaviors. In this case, a new executive-development program was only one of the HR systems needed—new compensation, selection, and performance-appraisal systems were designed to fit the new organization.

Getting clear definition of the elements of a development program kept this person from wasting time and money on an ill-defined program that at best might get high marks for entertainment but that, at worst, could detract from the credibility of the HR function. We are not suggesting that every call can or should be answered with an organization redesign, from strategy to selection. But HR professionals must continuously work to clarify the links between the elements of the process.

The following example illustrates another request for a program, but one with a purpose so clearly defined that the HR person could begin almost immediately to work on designing it:

> This call came to the HR person during the drive home after working late on a Friday evening. The VP-HR would like the individual to come up with a development program for divisional HR people. The VP had taken seriously an article in that morning's *Wall Street Journal*; re-engineering was beginning to consider the human side, and Mike Hammer and Jim Champy (*Wall Street Journal*, Tuesday January 17, 1995, page B1, "Managing Your Career" by Hal Lancaster) said that the first part of the changing relationship between employer and employee, which they referred to as a "new social contract" was that even though companies were no longer going to guarantee people a job, they were going to invest in their development so that they could become "something more." The VP-HR wanted a program that would contribute to better performance, but he recognized that their top performers could always command more pay; a development program that enabled them to be something more would prevent them from going somewhere else.
>
> Both the VP-HR and the HR person had a sound appreciation of the program-development elements in their company; the HR person over the weekend began networking with her professional contacts in other companies to generate ideas for the Monday morning session.

Given clear definition of the other elements of the process—the program purpose and expected outcomes—we can begin to define the behaviors to be developed.

Behaviors to Be Developed

A program of development is a process designed to help participants improve existing skills or learn new skills that will serve an organization's purpose. Decisions about which behaviors, skills, and frames of reference are desired as outcomes of a program of development are critical because they dictate the program that will be designed. These behaviors are the target that we are asking participants to shoot for.

There are two major issues surrounding identification of the behaviors targeted for development: (1) getting organizational acceptance of the behaviors chosen for development, that is, is this the right skill set?; and (2) using an appropriate method for determining what behaviors are needed.

Consider this actual case regarding the first:

> The consultant recommended that 200 executives be interviewed in order to determine the management and leadership skills of the future that would be required to take the company through the years ahead. The interviews targeted the issues facing the company, what skills it had and which ones it lacked. The "competencies of the future," reported after 200 interviews (and $100,000+), were remarkably similar to readily available competency lists and were considered too bland and generic to be of much more than general interest. The report was rejected as not very useful, and executive development was shelved until further notice. A new training director was brought in to review the effort.

Whatever the validity of the results described in this study, the effort did not develop the "buy-in" required to sustain confidence in the project. The individual interview process precluded group-level understanding of the link between business strategy, skills needed to accomplish that strategy, and the role of a program of development in teaching those skills. Money spent developing the tailored list might have been better spent creating processes to build acceptance of a reliable and valid generic list.

Compare the above case with another example:

> The CEO appointed a task force of high-potential executives, with support from HR, and hired an outside consultant to review the company's executive development efforts and to design the processes that would result in the required skills needed to meet the organization's strategy. One of the early actions of the task force was for high-potentials to conduct interviews with executives throughout the organization to relate strategy to needed executive behaviors.

Needless to say, organizational buy-in for the task force's results was not a problem. In fact, buy-in was built into the process for gathering the data. HR was not faced with trying to sell a solution—it was faced with trying to meet demands that the results be implemented immediately.

What is the key to acceptance of the results in the two examples? The important word is *ownership*. People believe and act upon conclusions that are reached through their own efforts or those of people they trust. Building participation of organizational partners into the design process is the surest means of gaining acceptance for the results.

The second issue is finding the appropriate method for determining the participant behaviors targeted for development. At each end of the spectrum are two basic approaches: armchairing and job analysis. The armchair method, as its name suggests, involves having a group of well-informed senior executives speculate about what behaviors, skills, and points of view future executives will need to get the results desired. The advantages of this approach are that it can be fast, inexpensive, easily understood, and acceptable to the organization. The disadvantages are that it may not be credible and the supposedly well-informed may simply be wrong. They may generate a list of behaviors that, in truth, only describe themselves, or they may generate a list of traits describing a very nice person. Unfortunately, these traits may fail to distinguish between executive effectiveness and ineffectiveness.

Job analysis, at the other end of the spectrum, uses systematic research processes to produce reliable, valid results that transcend the personal opinions of particular individuals. Its advantages are that it can be reliable, valid, and defensible to a court of law or other interested party. Its disadvantages are that it can be slow, expensive, poorly understood, and seen as not realistic.

A third strategy is to adopt an existing research-based model of effectiveness and bring it into the organization. The advantage of this method is that there is validity evidence for a chosen model, and time is not lost in developing the model. The disadvantage is getting buy-in; every company believes that it is unique and different, and general models may not seem to fit every organization the same or equally well.

Another issue in defining target behaviors is whether they focus in on the present or the future: Are we asking the participants to develop skills for today's or tomorrow's organization? There are well-developed job-analysis procedures for determining the skills required on current jobs. Identifying leadership and managerial skills for a future point in time—for example, what will high-potentials need to be able to do in five or ten years?—is more difficult. The usual content-validation strategy is not appropriate in this case. It is a static concept being employed for a dynamic situation. However, there are methods available (Spencer & Spencer, 1993) to tie anticipated business problems and challenges to a likely skill set. These methods involve, for example, identifying the business conditions and strategic initiatives that future executives will have to face and using subject matter experts to infer the skills that would be required for success under such conditions.

Whatever method is used, a key question is whether to use a set of behaviors specific to your organization or whether to adopt a more general model based on research across a number of companies. The pitfall to avoid is engaging in an endless and expensive search for the perfect competency model to fit your organization. Horror stories abound of companies who became embroiled in the quest for the perfect model. Not only is there a danger in investing in a static model that may be so organization specific that it will be obsolete tomorrow, but so much time and money can be spent in the competency search that little energy or momentum is left for actual development. Our caution is—don't spend all of your time, money, goodwill, and resources on building the competency model. Gain acceptance for your process, not the list.

Once the desired behaviors have been identified, the next step is to concentrate on understanding how to develop them.

The Model of Change

As an HR professional, your company-specific knowledge enables you to understand at each step of the way how a program of development will or can work in your company. Your core human-resources-development knowledge informs you as to what types of programs are likely to produce what types of behavior change, what research and experience in other organizations has produced, what things cost, and so forth.

Helping individuals develop targeted behaviors is the core of your program—the content and processes used to support the acquisition of an improved or new skill set and frame of reference. We address this topic here because what is possible in Step 5 (developmental strategies) will be determined by the model of change imbedded in the behaviors you choose to develop. Program purpose, desired outcomes, and the behaviors chosen as developmental targets will dictate the design of your program. Understanding how these behaviors are learned will dictate the content of individual development plans.

One key point in this report is that the program of development you design—the change element of your program—is bounded by the behaviors or outcomes you desire. And yet, this link between the program proposed and the actual behaviors, skills, or attitudes it can develop is often ignored in the design process.

In this section we will describe four types of programs to illustrate how program goals dictate the behaviors to be targeted and, thus, influence design.

The first type an organization may choose is an ongoing career-development program to increase employee satisfaction for all employees at a certain level by showing them how to take responsibility for their own careers. It is designed to help employees assess their skills and values in the context of their personal career goals. The program provides individuals with information about their interests, values, and skills through some kind of instrumented survey or feedback mechanism (e.g., Campbell, 1992; Schein, 1978; Strong, 1943) and also informs employees about the jobs available, the job-posting system, and the philosophy of the organization regarding tenure and promotion from within. Employees are expected to take the information about themselves and the organization and use this to implement a personal career plan.

In this type of program, career development is translated to mean, "What are my skills? What is it that I want to do in my career and how can I go about accomplishing my personal goals?" In those organizations moving toward a new employee relationship (one that does not promise job security and long-term employment) a career-development program is one way of helping employees assure employability, although not necessarily in their current organization. The program, as designed, may reasonably be expected to increase employee satisfaction—the program goal—if employees feel a greater sense of control over their own career destiny after completing it.

The second type of development program may be designed for the purpose of insuring that all participants at a certain level acquire the essential skills for effective performance in their current position. The skills to be developed are determined through the adoption of an existing research-based model of management (Byham, 1982; Kaplan, 1993; Yukl, Wall, & Lepsinger, 1990) or through conducting a job analysis (Levine, 1982; Tornow & Pinto, 1976). A job-analysis procedure insures that the skills to be developed are the ones the job requires and establishes content validity. The phrase *content validity* means that people who develop the requisite skills will manage better in a given job than people who do not develop the skills because the job requires those skills.

Examples of skills addressed in this type of program might include administrative skills such as running a meeting or scheduling; communication skills such as public-speaking or business-writing; or supervisory skills such as coaching, delegating, stress management, and time management.

There is evidence that many of these content-based skills can be taught in the classroom and learned in an environment that supports opportunities to practice and receive feedback on new behaviors (e.g., Goldstein & Sorcher, 1974). The organizational purpose is served if the majority of managers can demonstrate these skills as acquired through a combination of training, practice, and feedback and if the managers who have acquired these skills are indeed better managers.

Third, an organization may wish to create a program to develop the more complex cognitive, interpersonal, and personal capacities that are the knowledge, skills, and abilities executives will need at some future point in time as they move to positions of greater responsibility and accountability (Lombardo & McCauley, 1988). These skills are often addressed in succession-planning programs or as part of an initiative to change the culture of the organization. Many of these skills are not learned primarily in the classroom but are learned from experiences that include challenging assignments, working with other people who are very good (or very bad) at what they do, and coping with hardship and turmoil. In this case the development strategy and the program design shift from the classroom to a prescriptive strategy of providing assignment-based opportunities where skills can be learned.

Finally, the organization may design a program of development for the very senior members of the organization. Although these participants will probably have mastered the basic skills of management and have rich histories evidencing success in a variety of complex and challenging experiences, they often need help in obtaining straight feedback about the impact of their words and behavior on very large systems (Kaplan, 1985). They may need highly skilled and individual coaching assistance in wrestling with the very strengths that allowed them to be successful but are now causing them difficulty (Kaplan, 1991).

The good program designer understands how different skills are most likely acquired. In the four descriptions above we have illustrated four types of change strategies—giving information, coursework, learning from experience, and individualized coaching. The change strategy was imbedded in the skills to be learned and the skills were imbedded in the program purpose and desired outcomes.

One of our development principles is that the odds of success in a development program increase to the extent that its design is aligned with the skills to be developed. Another principle is that the program addresses behaviors and skills that can be developed. The odds for success go down considerably if underlying abilities, or personality characteristics, that change only with difficulty, if at all, are addressed. In other words, a program of development will not typically confront deep-seated personality issues unless it is designed to increase self-awareness. Then it might include feedback about personality characteristics and personal impact so that an individual can attempt to monitor and perhaps modify that impact. For example:

Very shy people might discover that their peers describe them as aloof, insensitive and isolated, not team-players. While shy folks are unlikely to become raging extraverts, they can adopt tactics to better manage the impression that others have of them. They may let others know that they are shy. They may learn how to become better listeners and become skilled at getting others to talk about themselves. They may take more time to simply "hang out" with others even if they still don't talk very much.

For more information, see:

Eastman, L. J. (1995). *Succession planning: An annotated bibliography and summary of commonly reported organizational practices.* Greensboro, NC: Center for Creative Leadership.

Lombardo, M. M., & Eichinger, R. W. (1989). *Preventing derailment: What to do before it's too late.* Greensboro, NC: Center for Creative Leadership.

Walker, J. W. (1980). *Human resource planning.* New York: McGraw-Hill.

STEP 3: Use Feedback as the Baseline for Executive Development

With the outline of our program in place, we turn to feedback— generating energy and providing direction for development. Both individuals and organizations have a natural tendency to seek the status quo, to try to maintain the comfortable, familiar style that has brought them success in the past. An executive development program, however, asks the target executives to break out of their familiar patterns in the service of better performance. That is not always an easy sell. The energy for change begins with dissatisfaction in the executive—the dissatisfaction that can come from feedback.

Feedback is an essential step in a program of development. It tells the executive where he or she stands against the set of behaviors that the organization has agreed need to be developed. The difficulty comes when the feedback event becomes confused with the program of development. Note that in our model feedback comes in the middle of the process; it does not stand alone.

Feedback involves participants comparing themselves against some standard; the greater the discrepancy between where they are and where they want to be (the standard), the greater the energy for change. The feedback must be seen by the participant as important, credible, and useful. It must be centered on those targeted behaviors discussed in the last section that are linked to program purpose, organizational outcomes, and business need. The feedback must imply action steps that are doable and that have important consequences. These requirements add up to the necessary conditions for developmental feedback.

Necessary Conditions for Developmental Feedback

Each of us receives feedback daily, but only occasionally do we receive feedback that helps us develop. What are the characteristics of that developmental feedback?

Credibility. Developmental feedback must be accurate and honest; it must come from those we are confident are qualified to comment on our performance. The essence of credibility is that those providing ratings or commentary on the performance of the executive must be competent to provide the data. Competence includes the opportunity to observe and the knowledge to attach meaning to the behavior. If the feedback designed into your development program is not credible to those on the receiving end, it will not generate much energy for change.

Meaning. Part of being meaningful is that the feedback results are interpretable—that they are in a form that makes sense to the executive; that he or she can understand the messages in the feedback.

Potential. Development implies change, so developmental feedback must address what the individual can do something about—things he or she can either change or compensate for. Nothing is so frustrating as to receive extensive feedback about something we can't do much about.

Confidentiality and anonymity. Feedback reported confidentially is more likely to be accepted (Burd & Ryan, 1993). Our experience verifies that research finding—participants respond less defensively when they are the owners of the data. A common rule-of-thumb is that the feedback is the property of the participant, but the development plan based on the feedback is shared between the participant and the manager.

Confidentiality is a hard sell in organizations where managers believe that people only change under threat of reprisal or punishment: "If we don't know what the report says, how can we make them change?" "The company is paying for the assessments—we have a right to know what they say." Our response is to reflect on the purpose of the development program—if your purpose is development. Development requires that the participant assume ownership of the need for change; participants are much more likely to assume ownership if the feedback data are confidential. Data gathered for developmental purposes are of higher quality and more accurate when raters believe that their ratings of a colleague, direct report, or boss will not be used to hurt them (Farh, Cannella, & Bedeian, 1991; Hazucha, Szymanski, & Birkeland, 1992).

Collecting data anonymously is a key issue. Research supports the commonsense observation that we take into account whether or not we will be identified personally when we give feedback. Bosses, subordinates, and peers are justifiably cautious in giving negative feedback when they have to personally explain it to the executive.

The downside of anonymity is that it can free us from accountability for what we say. An insensitive or hostile colleague can use the feedback to hurt the executive or to settle old scores. Especially when using written comments, some organizations provide a *quality screen* to assure that comments are within the bounds of civility.

Timeliness. Feedback loses credibility the longer the gap between being collected and reported back. In today's dynamic world, probably the outside limit between collecting and feeding back the data is about three months. After that, like yesterday's *Wall Street Journal,* it's "old news." Feedback should be provided as soon as possible.

Developmental feedback is designed to generate energy for change and to indicate what directions change should take. Your own organization must think through the necessary conditions for developmental feedback in its particular milieu. We suggest, however, that most of you will find the principles we listed are the basics to be built upon. Now we discuss specific ways to provide feedback.

Feedback Methods

Feedback can be as simple as a conversation between the manager and the participant or as complex as an assessment-center experience lasting several days. We will consider both the feedback instruments and the feedback provider. The instruments are the questionnaires, tests, and surveys that provide the data. The feedback provider has a special and critical role as the messenger, bringing the news to participants and helping them find meaning in the results.

The feedback instruments. The variety of instruments that may be used as feedback tools includes psychological tests such as ability and personality tests, self-inventories, employee-attitude surveys, structured or unstructured interviews in the organization, and paper-and-pencil questionnaires completed by others in the organization. Although all of these may be appropriate in particular circumstances, it will come as no surprise to participants in the Tools program that our focus here will be on multi-rater or 360-degree-feedback tools.

The popularity of the 360-degree-feedback process reflects its very useful aspects. It is relatively inexpensive and easy to administer; it provides a rare opportunity to see ourselves as others see us; and it offers the many perspectives of those in our 360-degree-feedback circle—bosses, peers, direct reports, customers, and so forth.

What instrument should be used? It depends on the purpose of the program. We have described different purposes as different targets that companies have used for the change (Hollenbeck, 1994); and different targets require different instruments. One target, better management, aims to develop managers toward a set of characteristics that define better management. Other programs aim directly at better job performance (for example, responds quickly to requests) and may simply ask customers how the executive can improve; others use 360-degree feedback as part of a strategic effort to set new dimensions of the company culture. Each type of program uses feedback to provide energy and direction for change, and in each case a different instrument is appropriate.

A basic question is whether to use a published or a "homemade" instrument. Although either can be well done, the competent published instrument will have survived a difficult set of standards. It will carry with it research demonstrating its reliability, validity, and usefulness that enables the user to evaluate it as a measuring instrument. Van Velsor and Leslie (1991a, 1991b) provided a set of guidelines for choosing a published instrument, as well as reviews of sixteen widely used instruments.

Issues to consider when choosing amongst published instruments include the costs to buy and deliver the instrument in time and dollars; its fit with the company culture; the amount of publisher support for the instrument such as development guides, the inclusion of test manuals, the availability of training in its use; and how well the instrument captures the behaviors being emphasized as desirable in your program.

Homemade instruments can be designed to meet very specific, immediate needs of a particular organization. How well they meet the standards of measurement will depend on the competence and care of the instrument developers. Seldom will an internal instrument be as rigorous a measurement instrument as those reviewed by Van Velsor and Leslie (1991a, 1991b), nor will they have the research database.

However, just as we emphasized in the discussion on executive behaviors, it is important not to get bogged down in the development of a homemade instrument. The trade-off between using an existing reliable and valid instrument that captures 85 percent of your internal model or using an internally developed instrument that may or may not be reliable and valid is evident. To build a program of development around an instrument that is neither reliable nor valid is a waste of time, money, and goodwill. To ask individuals to struggle to learn a set of behaviors that may or may not be related to effectiveness is to waste their time. However you go about choosing a feedback tool, be sure that the scores are related to effectiveness in some sensible way.

The feedback provider. Social science research tells us that feedback is most likely to be accepted by an executive when the feedback-giver is perceived as credible, competent, and trustworthy. In practical terms this means that organizations need to decide if they are going to use external or internal feedback-givers, and if they choose to go with internals, how they are going to prepare them.

The internal feedback-giver must be someone out of the executive's management chain and someone who is acknowledged by the organization as trustworthy, able to keep private information private. The internal or external feedback-giver must be experienced in giving feedback and be certified in the use of the particular instrument. One of the better programs that we know of provides internal feedback-givers with two days of training on how to use the instrument of choice and three days of training on coaching and interviewing techniques.

Some organizations give individual participants a choice of using an internal or external feedback-giver. When given the choice, most participants use the internal person.

The feedback-giver should be viewed as the bridge between the participant and the manager. Once the feedback has been given and a development plan has been drafted, the feedback-giver hands off the process to the manager who supports the participant in the implementation of the development plan.

In some cases the feedback-giver may be called upon to facilitate the development discussion with the boss or to help the participant seek additional feedback from some of the raters. In most cases the feedback-giver is the facilitator of the process. The individual and his or her manager are accountable for acting on the results.

Who Changes as a Result of Feedback?

Participants who receive feedback most discrepant from their own self-image of performance are those who change the most (Atwater, Roush, & Fischthal, 1992; Van Velsor, Ruderman, & Young, 1990). The dissatisfaction that comes from discovering that others see us much differently than we see ourselves can be a powerful motivater. Conger (1992) found that those most disappointed by feedback were found to be working hard to get better; those pleasantly surprised gained a boost in confidence that encouraged them to apply their talents more broadly. Maurer and Tarulli (1994) found that executives whose career is central to their identity believe that they are able to change, believe that they need skill development, have a career plan, and are most likely to engage in developmental activities.

Not surprisingly, as we will address in more detail in the next section, executives whose bosses support their change efforts are more likely to change (Hazucha, Hezlett, & Schneider, 1993; Maurer & Tarulli, 1994). And those in organizations with policies, rules, and guidelines that support development are likely to engage in such activities (Maurer & Tarulli, 1994).

Seldom have we seen a participant who is totally satisfied with his or her feedback results. On the other hand, seldom have we seen a set of results that doesn't offer some good news and hope for the future. More change takes place when the individual can see the payoff for his or her personal career goals. Managing the response to feedback is an important role of the feedback provider.

STEP 4: Define and Communicate the Critical Role of the Manager

We have placed responsibility for development squarely on the shoulders of the participant. This does not, however, diminish the critical role of the participant's manager, who is a critical link in the development process. Those who would design and implement a successful development-planning program must take responsibility for helping managers understand what roles they must play and how to play them.

The Manager's Role

Managers must make development real, provide developmental experiences, provide support and feedback, and provide access to organizational resources.

Make development real. The manager has a critical role in making development count for the executive and the organization. When development makes a difference in the performance of the executive and the organization, it suddenly becomes very real for the executive. Our development model depends on the manager to make that link. Managers know what work needs to be done and how the participant's development can contribute. They comprise the critical element that can take development in a vacuum and link it to business results.

We believe that managers fail in this task because development has so often been thought of as "training," that they despair that it will have any effect on business results or the participant. By demanding that the development plan offered by the participant show a clear relation to the work of the organization, the manager makes development real as well as communicates to the participant that development is important.

Provide developmental experiences. The participant's development depends on experiences, and the manager has the most direct impact on what experiences he or she gets. As the experience gatekeeper, the manager can open the door to new tasks, opportunities for interacting with new people, new business ventures, or he or she can wittingly or not prevent the participant from getting the experiences that develop.

Although the manager usually has a role in what new job assignments a participant will get, much of development will be development in place without a change in jobs. Unless managers think of development in place as a critical source of learning experiences and see their roles as helping participants use these, a major source of development is lost. Managers must be shown how to see the developmental challenge in every assignment and how to coach for task and process outcomes. An executive who must turn around sales can also use that opportunity to learn how to delegate more effectively. An executive assigned to troubleshoot a problem in currency exchange in Europe can also learn how to develop appreciation for people who see the world differently.

The whole process of development is really about teaching others how to learn. If the manager and the participant start to understand how to identify and benefit from the challenges imbedded in every opportunity, the half-life of developmental interventions will be of many years duration. Orienting the manager about how development works will spill over beyond the immediate participant and his or her development plan.

HR's responsibility is to help the manager break set, assume a new frame, to think of day-to-day work experiences as learning opportunities that can be coordinated with development plans.

Provide support and feedback. Learning new skills is seldom easy, and feedback is not a one-shot process. The manager often is in the best position to provide the needed support and the day-to-day feedback to the participant. Stories of individuals who benefited from programs of development feature managers who cared, who took the time and had the skills to provide support and ongoing feedback.

Provide access to organizational resources. Developmental opportunities abound in most organizations. Managers with the reputation of being "people developers" know where the opportunities are and how to access them. They know other managers willing and capable of teaching or coaching; they know what HR support is available; and they know how to influence assignment decisions so that both the participant and the organization will profit.

Enlisting the Manager

Getting a development-planning program underway requires bringing on board the managers who will serve these primary roles in development. Unless they understand the importance and duties of their roles and unless they buy into the program, results are likely to be sketchy at best.

How do we make it happen? How do we get them on board? First, we have an education task. Many managers have never thought of their development roles quite so specifically. They haven't thought about how critical their task is, the dynamics of how development takes place, or how to access organizational resources. They may not have the planning, support, and feedback skills required to be comfortable in their roles.

In addition to development education in general, we have a program-specific education task. Managers must know what the program is, what is expected of them, what results the program is expected to produce, and why they should participate.

How to accomplish the on-boarding task? It usually starts with a memo of support from senior management, followed by one-on-one sessions with managers who will participate. The outline for those meetings typically includes the roles listed here. This up-front time spent with managers is well worth the effort, but it is just the beginning. They will need continuing support if they are to carry out their roles in developing the participants.

STEP 5: Write the Development Plan

The steps in creating a development process—obtaining support and clarity of purpose, aligning the behaviors to be developed with that purpose, providing the target population with feedback against a standard, defining and supporting the role of the manager in the process—all lead to the next step, helping each individual who is a part of the process create a viable plan for acting on the feedback. In this section we will describe the elements of an effective plan for individual development; the roles played by the human resources professional, the manager, and the participant in writing and executing these plans; and the organizational context that nourishes and supports development.

The Elements of an Effective Plan

A well-conceived development plan is the link between an individual's motivation to acquire new skills and the work of the organization. It is a description of what a person intends to do in order to become more effective and how he or she intends to go about it. An individual development plan is a tool that illustrates the steps one will take to learn new skills in response to feedback.

Development plans may be as simple as scribbles on a blank sheet of paper or as complex as a computer-generated document of prescriptions. The essence of a plan for individual development is not the form nor the technology. They err who seek copies of a company's development-planning form and believe that they have captured the process. The essence of the plan is the extent to which it engages the individual to embark upon a journey of personal growth.

An effective plan includes these elements: a development goal or objective; developmental strategies (action steps) with milestones; and standards against which to measure progress. The process is built on the premise that adults learn best what the situation demands.

The development goal. The first step in creating a plan is to determine the development goal. A viable goal is congruent with an individual's sense of his or her own performance and work experience over time. "This is an issue I really need to tackle; I can't ignore it any longer. I've heard it before from more than one person in more than one situation." A viable goal reflects an individual's own career goals. For example, individuals who do not aspire to become general managers will not be interested in development goals that move them in that direction. The goal must reflect direction and ownership. It must point toward a behavior change that will serve the executive and the organization. It must serve the career aspirations of the executive and the business need of the company or work group.

What happens when a participant does not choose the goal that the manager or the HR professional believes he or she should choose? No matter how much the HR professional or manager believes the person needs to change a particular behavior, if the individual does not own the goal, development will not occur. Program designers need to recall the concept of readiness. Individuals will attempt to change what they are ready to change. The goal they choose may not seem important to the onlooker, but it represents the degree of dissonance and imperfection that the person can tolerate at a point in time. Individuals may have to achieve small successes with seemingly lesser goals before they can take on some of the bigger issues.

What makes a good development goal? Better goals are more concrete, and are expressed in terms of specific behaviors. The behaviors may lead to business results, but development focuses on the behaviors, not the results.

We found a very useful tool for defining those behaviors in use at the General Electric Corporation (see Figure 1). Informally called the *Bull's Eye,* it is used to help an individual or group take abstract, sometimes ill-defined ideas and translate them into concrete behaviors.

When GE CEO Jack Welch identifies a desirable executive characteristic—for instance, "global mind"—executives can use the Bull's Eye to make the concept concrete and behavioral. The exercise would ask, "What does a global mind look like in terms of behaviors? If we are to have a global mind at year end, what will we be doing new or more of, and what will we be doing less of?" This simple exercise can be remarkably effective in defining the goal.

Here is an example of one executive's experience with the exercise (the specific list of behaviors for this executive is filled in on Figure 1):

> The executive's primary need was to learn to tolerate ambiguity during the team consensus-building process. The facilitator brought the target to identify a list of behaviors in the executive's job that would indicate the ability to tolerate ambiguity. The list was long and specific. Some of the items were:
> - Listen for two additional minutes beyond the impulse to say something.
> - Ask clarifying questions instead of giving own point of view.
> - Identify colleague who will signal you every time you interrupt.
> - Keep a tally of each comment that represents a push for closure rather than a clarification.

Even the executive had to admit that there was nothing on the list that he couldn't do. And once the list was in place, what it meant to tolerate ambiguity took on a new, and achievable, meaning.

How many goals should a development plan include? Not many. Most executives find that one or two or three significant goals are about all that can be addressed at any one time—both in terms of time available and focus.

Developmental strategies. After a goal has been set the participant needs to determine how to address it. Based on the lessons-of-experience

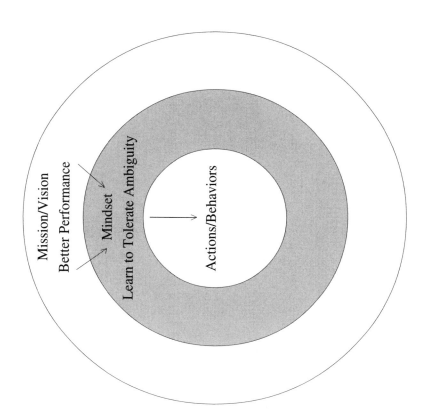

I.
Mission/Vision

II.
Desired Behavioral Changes

More of . . .
1. Listen for two additional minutes.
2. Ask clarifying questions.

Less of . . .
1. Push for closure.
2. Interrupt.

Bull's Eye reproduced with permission of Steve Kerr, Chief Learning Officer, GE Leadership Development Institute.

Making Missions Actionable

Mission/Vision
Better Performance
Mindset
Learn to Tolerate Ambiguity
Actions/Behaviors

Figure 1
Change Acceleration Process: Defining Performance

research at CCL (see McCall et al., 1988), there are four possible developmental strategies for the executive to consider: learning from work assignments and tasks, learning from others, learning from hardships, and coursework/reading. It is the job of the HR professional to introduce these strategies to the participants.

If possible, it is best to build the developmental strategy right into the work situation, using either the participant's current job or, if warranted, negotiating a change in assignment. Because the learning is tied to the work, there is a greater likelihood that the participant will follow through on the plan and that the manager will support the plan. For example:

> A manager has learned from her feedback that her direct reports do not feel that she provides them with visibility or recognition. Additionally, even though she works late hours and produces an enormous amount of work, she has been rated by her boss as a person that lacks the strategic perspective of senior managers. This is a shock since she believes that she is very strategic. Finally, sales in the SE region of the company, one of her regions, are dropping off. Based on her feedback, this manager writes the following development goals: (1) To be perceived by senior management as able to think and act strategically, and (2) to provide direct reports with visibility and recognition. As her developmental strategy she decides to design a plan to turn around the sales situation in the SE. If she pulls this off successfully she will be able to develop and demonstrate her strategic abilities. To accomplish this, she will have to delegate more of her work to her direct reports, and as a part of this delegation will work to give them visibility and recognition. To help keep her from falling back into her old patterns of doing it all herself, she will identify someone in her immediate work environment who can help her monitor her efforts and let her know if she is backsliding. She will share her plan with her boss and ask the boss to coach her in this effort.

This real-world plan is not in addition to work. It *is* the work. But it is using the work as the classroom to learn and practice new skills. It is unlikely to be set aside because there is real work to do. The development plan becomes the tool that helps participants and managers understand how learning occurs. When focused learning can occur in the individual's current job, in an activity valued by the organization, moving the individual in the career direction he or she wants to go, it is magic. The individual is motivated to learn. The opportunity exists. The organization supports the effort. In this situation you do not hear, "I did not have time to work on my development plan."

For a work assignment to be used as a developmental strategy it must provide the participant with the opportunity to grapple with unfamiliar responsibilities and to prove him- or herself. The participant must be stretched in new ways but not be so overloaded that stress overwhelms the opportunity to learn. It is important in using assignments as developmental experiences to be sure that the individual is in the assignment long enough to understand the job, make some decisions, understand the consequences of his or her decisions, and correct mistakes.

A second developmental strategy is learning from others. As described by McCauley and Young in 1993, relationship-based learning provides some mixture of motivation, opportunity, and support. Coaches and role models are two examples of relationships that provide these three ingredients.

Coaches can help participants diagnose what needs to be done, find alternative strategies, and motivate them to stay on plan. They are especially helpful in serving as "nudges"—the regular reminder of what needs to be done and where we are in the change process. Effective coaches may be *designated coaches* in the HR function, outside consultants, or concerned others. Colleagues or friends may provide encouragement and also keep developing participants accountable, pointing out to them when they slip back into old habits and ways of doing things, as well as encouraging them when they try new things.

Because first attempts at using unfamiliar, unpracticed, or new skills will only be approximations of the desired outcome, the development plan needs to include some mechanism for the executive to solicit ongoing feedback about his or her attempts to practice and use the new skills. To provide feedback, others need to know what the target behaviors are and what types of feedback are needed.

A range of other people can serve as role models of the desired behaviors. A common technique is identifying someone else, usually a colleague or executive, who does really well what the participant wants to learn. Then by watching what the model does and what happens, participants learn how to do it themselves. Although the model is usually someone in the organization, anyone will do—a television announcer, a customer, a family member—as long as the executive has a chance to observe that person regularly. Modeling works best when the participant can identify with the model, usually when he or she is similar to the participant in some important characteristic. Modeling is particularly useful in delicate personal areas like dress or speech. What does the model do? How does he or she dress?

A third developmental strategy is learning from hardships. Although we do not recommend that you prescribe hardships when teaching individuals how to write their development plans, you may encounter someone who is entrenched in a hardship situation coincident to their involvement in the development program. It is important to note that learning may not seem to be taking place within the hardship situation because the person may feel too stressed and overwhelmed. The ability to articulate the learning from a hardship typically requires reflection some time after the hardship has passed and the executive has survived. However, it is possible that you can facilitate or accelerate this learning if you can help the executive cope with the stress and anxiety that accompanies the situation. Coping tactics include helping the executive identify those aspects of the situation that are within his or her control, offering tools for reflection and mechanisms of support. We include learning from hardships in this section not only because CCL's research (McCall et al., 1988; see, for example, chapter 4) cites it as an important source of executive learning, but because some portion of the executives you have in your program will be struggling with hardships of some kind. When that is the case, it is not the time to pile on more developmental opportunity. It is the time to help the participant take stock and cope.

A fourth developmental strategy is coursework and reading. When the development need reflects a lack of content knowledge (for example, time management, how to read a balance sheet, how to handle conflict negotiation, how to do public speaking) or a lack of self-awareness (for example, others perceive the participant as rude and insensitive but he or she doesn't know why), the plan should include a listing of the courses, books, and so forth that might address the particular need. The downside of coursework and reading is that in the experience of many managers and participants, attending courses has been the sum total of the development effort. Managers and participants should be reminded that coursework is useful as part of a total effort that involves other strategies.

Whatever strategy is employed, the person writing his or her own development plan needs to recognize that learning new skills requires using a variety of tactics, some of which may be pretty uncomfortable. For example, an individual who needs to learn how to put other people at ease might observe someone who is good at that, then read about how to make small talk and, finally, find someone to practice with. A person who is not good at putting others at ease may be inclined to neglect the last step.

Also, the understanding that how we learn is bound up with what we learn may provide executives with support for going against the grain of the comfortable and familiar in service to achievement of a development goal.

Finally, any journey requires milestones. Effective planning requires specific timetables and milestones for the action steps. Whatever developmental strategies are decided upon, the individual must attach a time frame to each action step—specifically, when and how the step will be completed. These milestones are motivational and let us know whether we are making progress.

Measurement standards. The summary elements of the development plan are progress measures. After we have completed the journey, has the objective been met? Has behavior changed? Has the executive developed? Measurement may be as simple as "judged by the manager," a re-administration of 360-degree feedback, or it might be passing the CPA exam. All goals should have some standard that closes the loop and enables the executive and the organization to determine whether the target development has taken place.

The Development-planning Roles

There are three development roles that, working together, make development happen: the role of the participant, the role of the manager, and the role of the development facilitator.

The different roles may be played by three different people or they may be combined, but each role has responsibilities.

The participant must assume ownership of his or her development needs, must do the self-analysis required to understand what development is needed, and must be committed to develop. The HR development person and the manager have a number of tools to help the participant understand what is required. Feedback is a basic tool to encourage ownership and analysis; commitment comes from aligning the participant's goals with the rewards of developing, or from a realization by the participant of the implications not developing may have on his or her career or performance.

A frequently asked question is, "How do we gain commitment to the process from the participant?" Simple direct feedback about how developing will help (or hurt) the participant achieve his or her goals is most effective. A commitment to change may be easy or hard to obtain, depending on how much the changes affect the participant's basic self view. One of the advantages of behavioral development goals is that they attack behaviors, not the person. That simple direct feedback should come first from data such as 360-degree feedback and then be reinforced by significant others (the manager or other important figures in the organization). If in fact there are no significant consequences for the participant in staying the same, then getting commitment to change will be extremely difficult.

The manager owns the responsibility to help the participant carry out the development plan. Although a very determined participant may be able to carry out the plan without the boss's help, development is difficult unless the manager supports it. This support can come through feedback, coaching, encouragement, and reward. Or it may come through access to resources, other people, or work opportunities that the participant alone may not be able to use.

Here's an example of what happens when the manager doesn't get on board:

> The company brought in the coach to facilitate the development of a senior executive whose leadership style was not seen by his new manager as adequate for the future demands of the job. The consultant dutifully worked with both executive and manager to produce a development plan that would produce results. The manager, however, for whatever reasons would not help with the development, instead leaving it to the facilitator and the executive. After months of floundering, both the facilitator and the executive declared the effort a failure.

Development facilitators bring optimism, insight, and opportunity to the process. They must bring the optimism that the process will work—an optimism that will motivate both the manager and the participant and carry the process along. They must be good listeners who are able to size up the situation; they must be helpful in generating action steps; and they must have the personal integrity to serve as a go-between for the manager and the participant, if required.

The Organization Context

Those who have attended our Tools program have seen, firsthand, the wide differences in how much an organization will support development. People development is a basic premise in some organizations. But even organizations that focus exclusively on short-term results are finding that a new employee-employer relationship is developing which calls for development opportunities to replace the promise of lifetime employment. A frequently heard phrase is, "We can't promise you employment, but we will promise you employability." Those seeking to implement development plans should carefully consider the context in which they work.

A developmental context is characterized by the following:
(1) Managers will be recognized, rewarded, and held accountable for the

development of their employees. (2) They will support multiple routes to development, for example, coaching, coursework, challenging work, and access to experts. Organizations that provide these multiple routes (including training, assignments, other people used as coaches, models, and mentors) report more positive outcomes (Shaeffer, 1984). (3) Development goals will be framed as efforts toward personal mastery rather than as performance outcomes. By this we mean that the emphasis is on the process rather than the outcome. For example, consider the following development goal—an individual has as his or her goal to listen more, interrupt less, and talk less in staff meetings. If the focus is on performance outcomes, then the first time the person is sitting in a meeting and interrupts, he or she has failed to achieve that goal. He or she may feel discouraged, embarrassed, and may just give it up as an unattainable goal. If the focus is on the process, then the person will perhaps have arranged for a colleague to provide feedback after every meeting about his or her progress, "better last week, not so good today." The individual may be keeping a learning log to reflect on the triggers that cause the interruption—so that the motivation behind the behavior will emerge. And the desired behavior change will—with fits and starts—finally become a part of the individual's repertoire. Performance outcomes lead to nonproductive evaluations of success or failure. Learning outcomes point toward under- standing and change; incorporate effort and successive approximations; and, most especially, provide support for the learning and understanding of how learning occurs. (4) In a developmental context, feedback and the opportunity to practice and learn new things will be construed as an essential part of the culture.

Designers of development programs can profit from spending some time reflecting on why past efforts have not succeeded. We provide below a list of common reasons we have garnered about why programs have not worked:

- Programs are designed with vague and global outcomes.
- Organizations are unwilling to commit the resources and time to support meaningful change.
- Change is difficult.
- Change takes time.
- The feedback activity is construed as the program.
- Development plans all say the same thing, "Take a course."

For more information, see:

Bunker, K., & Webb, A. (1992). *Learning how to learn from experience: Impact of stress and coping.* Greensboro, NC: Center for Creative Leadership.

McCall, M. W., Jr. (1988). *Developing executives through work experience.* Greensboro, NC: Center for Creative Leadership.

STEP 6: Make the Program Accountable

Development-planning programs are supported because they make a difference in critical ways. It is up to you to demonstrate that difference by collecting the data and doing the evaluation that convinces senior management that the program is worth the cost. Program evaluation may indeed be the "slough of despond." What is possible often falls far short of the desirable. There may be little interest in evaluation. The criteria may be difficult to agree on, much less measure.

Nonetheless, the long-term success of a development program (not to mention your own success) depends on demonstrating what value-added component the program brought. That value will be very organization specific—your criteria are not likely to be the same as those used in another organization. But there are common indicators, common evaluation processes, and common approaches to guide your efforts, as well as urge you on.

Whether it is even possible to evaluate your program will depend on the clarity of your program purpose and outcomes which, you will recall, was Step 2 of this process. For example, if the purpose of the program is to increase employee satisfaction, then some measure of employee satisfaction must be included as an outcome criterion. Likewise if the purpose of the program is to prepare high-potentials for promotion, then some measure of that must be a criterion reflecting, for example, whether high-potentials who go through the program get promoted when positions become available. The outcome measure must reflect program purpose.

However, outcome evaluations are more interpretable if you have built a process evaluation into your program and if you are able to fold those findings back into your program on a continuous basis. Consider the following two examples:

Fifteen people participated in an executive development program where they were provided with feedback, instructed on how to write a development plan, and asked to take the plan and meet with their boss as the first step toward implementation. Twelve months later, a post-test evaluation tool was administered. To the chagrin of all involved, very little change had occurred in these executives. The discouraged program sponsors withdrew their support, and shortly thereafter the program folded.

In a second company, the same feedback and action-planning took place, but three months after the event the program designers called all fifteen individuals to ask them if they had shared the plan with their boss and how the boss had responded. Five people said they had never met with their boss. Seven people said their boss had been either noncommittal or cynical about their plan. Three people reported an experience as anticipated by the program designers, which pointed to the need for changes to the program *before* bringing any more executives into the feedback process and before engaging in any post-program evaluation activity. The program designers changed the program to only allow participants in the program who had been nominated by their boss. They personally met with individual managers to help them frame their role, and they set up a three-way development plan meeting with the boss and the executive to facilitate the presentation and pass off the action plan to the line manager. They also created a course for the managers on how to coach and give feedback.

These examples illustrate that evaluating programs of development occurs on many levels. Evaluation is the last step in an existing program but is also the first step in the next program. Evaluation is outcome based—but to have interpretable outcomes, evaluation must also be process based.

However, evaluation is not only conducted at the organizational outcome and process level, it must also be conducted at the individual level.

At the individual level the program designer and the executive will probably want to know how much change has taken place from time one (perhaps when feedback was collected) to time two (six-to-eighteen months later). There are several ways to gather this information. The simplest method is to conduct interviews with the participants and their bosses, subordinates, or peers and ask them if the participant has changed in a particular direction. An important point to remember if you do interviews about a development goal is to obtain permission from the participant to talk to his or her boss, peers, and direct reports about the goal. One approach is to obtain this permission in writing during your initial program. In addition, you should guarantee the participants and those you interview both anonymity and confidentiality. While this method is the most straightforward, it is time-consuming.

A common evaluation method is to administer the 360-degree-feedback instrument a second time, after the executives have had a chance to develop. Simple to do, the results from such a testing are surprisingly difficult to interpret accurately. There are many statistical artifacts involved in pre/post tests that may mask real change. If your organization is large enough and receptive to a rigorous evaluation, you may want to do a formal evaluation—complete with control groups. Unless you are an evaluation expert you will want to get help with this methodology. Many vendors of training-and-development tools can provide (for a fee) help in designing a program evaluation. Assistance may also be available from a local college, either from the students, the faculty, or both.

Implementing and evaluating a program of development planning is time-consuming, difficult, and often the results are not immediately evident. One way to maintain the momentum in the organization (and yourself) is to take advantage of small wins. Set small, achievable milestones for your program rather than a global, long-term goal. A first goal might be to provide feedback to a group of executives to demonstrate to the organization that collecting and providing confidential data is possible. Your next goal might be to have a group of senior managers discuss the skill levels of their managers and define a program purpose, to increase the skills. Setting program design goals with evaluation and feedback is just as important as the more global goals that you set for the program overall and for the individuals in the program.

For more information, see:

McCauley, C. D., & Hughes-James, M. W. (1994). *An evaluation of the outcomes of a leadership development program.* Greensboro, NC: Center for Creative Leadership.

Conclusion

We trust that we've answered the question, "How do I actually design a development program?"—a question that is asked more and more frequently as organizations respond to an environment where work is changing faster than anyone could have imagined a few years ago. If we've actually answered it for you, then you should come away knowing that we believe that a development plan must be fundamental enough to cover the majority of development challenges yet solid enough to withstand the shifting trends of the workplace. *Simplicity* and *stability* should be the bywords.

With respect to simplicity, in today's organization much depends on learning what is most critical to know. That means that if you are in charge of developing others, your knowledge and experience are invaluable in finding and using the best information on how to effectively develop your organization's most valuable assets, its employees. Sifting through your and others' lessons of history to reduce them to their most important applicable aspects is daunting, but can be ultimately rewarding.

Simplicity leads to stability. We believe a basic, solid development plan is an island of stability in the ever-changing currents that challenge the modern organization. If you have in hand a set of principles that are concrete but flexible enough to be applied over time and can be easily modified to fit circumstance, you have the essentials to propel you through even the roughest patches of corporate capriciousness.

References

Atwater, L., Roush, P., & Fischthal, A. (1992). The influence of upward feedback on self and follower ratings of leadership. *Personnel Psychology, 48*(1), 35-59.

Burd, K. A., & Ryan, A. M. (1993). *Reactions to developmental feedback in an assessment center.* Paper presented at the eighth annual meeting of the Society for Industrial Organizational Psychology, San Francisco.

Byham, W. C. (1982). *Dimensions of managerial competence* (monograph VI). Pittsburgh: Developmental Dimensions International.

Campbell, D. P. (1992). *Campbell Interest and Skill Survey*™. Minneapolis: National Computer Systems.

Conger, J. A. (1992). *Learning to lead: The art of transforming managers into leaders.* San Francisco: Jossey-Bass.

Farh, J. L., Cannella, A. A., & Bedeian, A. G. (1991). Peer ratings: The impact of purpose on rating quality and user acceptance. *Group and Organizational Studies, 16*(4), 367-386.

Goldstein, A. P., & Sorcher, M. (1974). *Changing supervisor behavior.* New York: Pergamon.

Hazucha, J. T., Hezlett, S., & Schneider, R. J. (1993). The impact of 360-degree feedback on management skills development. *Human Resources Management, 32,* 325-352.

Hazucha, J. T., Szymanski, C., & Birkeland, S. (1992). *Will my boss see my ratings? Effect of confidentiality on self-boss rating congruence.* Paper presented at the 100th annual meeting of the American Psychological Association, Washington, D.C.

Hollenbeck, G. (1994). *Workshop on multisource feedback.* Paper presented at the annual meeting of the Society for Industrial Organizational Psychology, San Francisco.

Kaplan, R. (1985). *High hurdles: The challenge of executive self-development.* Greensboro, NC: Center for Creative Leadership.

Kaplan, R. (1991). *Beyond ambition: How driven managers can lead better and live better.* San Francisco: Jossey-Bass.

Kaplan, R. (1993). *SkillScope.* Greensboro, NC: Center for Creative Leadership.

Lancaster, H. (1995, January 17). Managing your career. *The Wall Street Journal,* p. B1.

Levine, E. (1982). *Everything you wanted to know about job analysis but was afraid to ask.* Tampa, FL: Mariner Press.

Lombardo, M., & McCauley, C. (1988). *Benchmarks.* Greensboro, NC: Center for Creative Leadership.

Maurer, T. J., & Tarulli, B. A. (1994). Investigation of perceived environment, perceived outcome, and person variable in relationship to voluntary development activity by employees. *Journal of Applied Psychology, 79*(1), 3-14.

McCall, M. W., Jr., Lombardo, M. M., & Morrison, A. M. (1988). *The lessons of experience: How successful executives develop on the job.* Lexington, MA: Lexington Books.

McCauley, C. D., Ruderman, M. N., Ohlott, P. J., & Morrow, J. (1994). Assessing the developmental components of managerial jobs. *Journal of Applied Psychology, 79*(4), 544-560.

McCauley, C. D., & Young, D. P. (1993). Creating developmental relationships: Roles and strategies. *Human Resources Management Review, 3*(3), 219-230.

Revans, R. W. (1980). *Action learning.* Great Britain: Anchor Press Ltd.

Schein, E. H. (1978). *Career dynamics: Matching individual and organizational needs.* Reading, MA: Addison-Wesley.

Seibert, K. W., Hall, D. T., & Kram, K. (1995). Strengthening the weak link in strategic executive development: Integrating individual development and global business strategy. *Human Resource Management, 34,* 529-547.

Shaeffer, R. G. (1984). Developing strategic leadership. *The Conference Board,* Report No. 847, pp. 40-41.

Spencer, L. M., Jr., & Spencer, S. M. (1993). *Competence at work: Models for superior performance.* New York: John Wiley.

Strong, E. K., Jr. (1943). *Strong Interest Inventory.* Palo Alto, CA: Consulting Psychologists Press.

Tornow, W. T., & Pinto, P. R. (1976). The development of a managerial job taxonomy: A system for describing, classifying, and evaluating executive positions. *Journal of Applied Psychology, 61*(4), 410-418.

Van Velsor, E., & Leslie, J. (1991a). *Feedback to managers, Volume 1: A guide to evaluating multi-rater feedback instruments.* Greensboro, NC: Center for Creative Leadership.

Van Velsor, E., & Leslie, J. (1991b). *Feedback to managers, Volume 2: A review and comparison of sixteen multi-rater feedback instruments.* Greensboro, NC: Center for Creative Leadership.

Van Velsor, E., Ruderman, M. N., & Young, D. P. (1990). *The impact of feedback on self-assessment and performance in three domains of managerial behavior.* Unpublished manuscript. Greensboro, NC: Center for Creative Leadership.

Wick, C. W., & León, L. S. (1993). *The learning edge: How smart managers and smart companies stay ahead.* New York: McGraw-Hill.

Yukl, G., Wall, S., & Lepsinger, R. (1990). Preliminary report on validation of the Managerial Practices Survey. In K. E. Clark & M. B. Clark (Eds.), *Measures of leadership.* West Orange, NJ: Leadership Library of America.

CENTER FOR CREATIVE LEADERSHIP PUBLICATIONS

SELECTED REPORTS:

The Adventures of Team Fantastic: A Practical Guide for Team Leaders and Members
G.L. Hallam (1996, Stock #172) $20.00
Beyond Work-Family Programs J.R. Kofodimos (1995, Stock #167) $25.00
CEO Selection: A Street-smart Review G.P. Hollenbeck (1994, Stock #164) $25.00
Coping With an Intolerable Boss M.M. Lombardo & M.W. McCall, Jr. (1984, Stock #305) $10.00
The Creative Opportunists: Conversations with the CEOs of Small Businesses
J.S. Bruce (1992, Stock #316) $12.00
Creativity in the R&D Laboratory T.M. Amabile & S.S. Gryskiewicz (1987, Stock #130) $12.00
The Dynamics of Management Derailment M.M. Lombardo & C.D. McCauley (1988, Stock #134). $12.00
Eighty-eight Assignments for Development in Place: Enhancing the Developmental
Challenge of Existing Jobs M.M. Lombardo & R.W. Eichinger (1989, Stock #136) $15.00
Enhancing 360-degree Feedback for Senior Executives: How to Maximize the Benefits and
Minimize the Risks R.E. Kaplan & C.J. Palus (1994, Stock #160) $15.00
An Evaluation of the Outcomes of a Leadership Development Program C.D. McCauley &
M.W. Hughes-James (1994, Stock #163) $35.00
Evolving Leaders: A Model for Promoting Leadership Development in Programs C.J. Palus &
W.H. Drath (1995, Stock #165) $20.00
Feedback to Managers, Volume I: A Guide to Evaluating Multi-rater Feedback Instruments
E. Van Velsor & J. Brittain Leslie (1991, Stock #149) $20.00
Feedback to Managers, Volume II: A Review and Comparison of Sixteen Multi-rater
Feedback Instruments E. Van Velsor & J. Brittain Leslie (1991, Stock #150) $80.00
Forceful Leadership and Enabling Leadership: You Can Do Both R.E. Kaplan (1996, Stock #171) $20.00
Gender Differences in the Development of Managers: How Women Managers Learn From
Experience E. Van Velsor & M. W. Hughes (1990, Stock #145) $35.00
A Glass Ceiling Survey: Benchmarking Barriers and Practices A.M. Morrison, C.T. Schreiber,
& K.F. Price (1995, Stock #161) $20.00
How to Design an Effective System for Developing Managers and Executives M.A. Dalton &
G.P. Hollenbeck (1996, Stock #158) $15.00
The Intuitive Pragmatists: Conversations with Chief Executive Officers J.S. Bruce
(1986, Stock #310) $12.00
Key Events in Executives' Lives E.H. Lindsey, V. Homes, & M.W. McCall, Jr.
(1987, Stock #132) $65.00
Leadership for Turbulent Times L.R. Sayles (1995, Stock #325) $20.00
Learning How to Learn From Experience: Impact of Stress and Coping K.A. Bunker &
A.D. Webb (1992, Stock #154) $30.00
A Look at Derailment Today: North America and Europe J. Brittain Leslie & E. Van Velsor
(1996, Stock #169) $25.00
Making Common Sense: Leadership as Meaning-making in a Community of Practice
W.H. Drath & C.J. Palus (1994, Stock #156) $15.00
Managerial Promotion: The Dynamics for Men and Women M.N. Ruderman, P.J. Ohlott, &
K.E. Kram (1996, Stock #170) $15.00
Off the Track: Why and How Successful Executives Get Derailed M.W. McCall, Jr., &
M.M. Lombardo (1983, Stock #121) $10.00
Perspectives on Dialogue: Making Talk Developmental for Individuals and Organizations
N.M. Dixon (1996, Stock #168) $20.00
Preventing Derailment: What To Do Before It's Too Late M.M. Lombardo &
R.W. Eichinger (1989, Stock #138) $25.00
The Realities of Management Promotion M.N. Ruderman & P.J. Ohlott (1994, Stock #157) $20.00
Redefining What's Essential to Business Performance: Pathways to Productivity,
Quality, and Service L.R. Sayles (1990, Stock #142) $20.00
Succession Planning: An Annotated Bibliography L.J. Eastman (1995, Stock #324) $20.00
Training for Action: A New Approach to Executive Development R.M. Burnside &
V.A. Guthrie (1992, Stock #153) $15.00
Traps and Pitfalls in the Judgment of Executive Potential M.N. Ruderman & P.J. Ohlott
(1990, Stock #141) $20.00
Twenty-two Ways to Develop Leadership in Staff Managers R.W. Eichinger & M.M. Lombardo
(1990, Stock #144) $15.00

Upward-communication Programs in American Industry A.I. Kraut & F.H. Freeman
(1992, Stock #152) $30.00
Using an Art Technique to Facilitate Leadership Development C. De Ciantis (1995, Stock #166)... $30.00
Why Executives Lose Their Balance J.R. Kofodimos (1989, Stock #137) $20.00
Why Managers Have Trouble Empowering: A Theoretical Perspective Based on
Concepts of Adult Development W.H. Drath (1993, Stock #155) $15.00

SELECTED BOOKS:
Balancing Act: How Managers Can Integrate Successful Careers and Fulfilling Personal Lives
J.R. Kofodimos (1993, Stock #247) $27.00
Beyond Ambition: How Driven Managers Can Lead Better and Live Better R.E. Kaplan,
W.H. Drath, & J.R. Kofodimos (1991, Stock #227) $29.95
Breaking the Glass Ceiling: Can Women Reach the Top of America's Largest Corporations?
(Updated Edition) A.M. Morrison, R.P. White, & E. Van Velsor (1992, Stock #236A) $13.00
Choosing to Lead (Second Edition) K.E. Clark & M.B. Clark (1996, Stock #327) $25.00
Developing Diversity in Organizations: A Digest of Selected Literature A.M. Morrison &
K.M. Crabtree (1992, Stock #317) $25.00
Discovering Creativity: Proceedings of the 1992 International Creativity and Innovation
Networking Conference S.S. Gryskiewicz (Ed.) (1993, Stock #319) $30.00
Executive Selection: A Look at What We Know and What We Need to Know
D.L. DeVries (1993, Stock #321) $20.00
Healing the Wounds: Overcoming the Trauma of Layoffs and Revitalizing Downsized
Organizations D.M. Noer (1993, Stock #245) $27.50
If I'm In Charge Here, Why Is Everybody Laughing? D.P. Campbell (1984, Stock #205) $8.95
If You Don't Know Where You're Going You'll Probably End Up Somewhere Else
D.P. Campbell (1974, Stock #203) $9.40
Inklings: Collected Columns on Leadership and Creativity D.P. Campbell (1992, Stock #233)....... $15.00
Leadership Education 1996-1997: A Source Book (Sixth Edition), Vol. 1, Leadership Courses
and Programs F.H. Freeman, K.B. Knott, & M.K. Schwartz (Eds.) (1996, Stock #330) $35.00
Leadership Education 1996-1997: A Source Book (Sixth Edition), Vol. 2, Leadership Resources
F.H. Freeman, K.B. Knott, & M.K. Schwartz (Eds.) (1996, Stock #331) $35.00
Leadership: Enhancing the Lessons of Experience (Second Edition) R.L. Hughes, R.C. Ginnett,
& G.J. Curphy (1996, Stock #266) $49.95
The Lessons of Experience: How Successful Executives Develop on the Job M.W. McCall, Jr.,
M.M. Lombardo, & A.M. Morrison (1988, Stock #211) $22.95
Making Diversity Happen: Controversies and Solutions A.M. Morrison, M.N. Ruderman, &
M. Hughes-James (1993, Stock #320) $25.00
The New Leaders: Guidelines on Leadership Diversity in America A.M. Morrison
(1992, Stock #238) $29.00
Readings in Innovation S.S. Gryskiewicz & D.A. Hills (Eds.) (1992, Stock #240) $25.00
Selected Research on Work Team Diversity M.N. Ruderman, M.W. Hughes-James, &
S.E. Jackson (Eds.) (1996, Stock #326) $24.95
Take the Road to Creativity and Get Off Your Dead End D.P. Campbell (1977, Stock #204) $8.95
Whatever It Takes: The Realities of Managerial Decision Making (Second Edition)
M.W. McCall, Jr., & R.E. Kaplan (1990, Stock #218) $30.40
The Working Leader: The Triumph of High Performance Over Conventional Management
Principles L.R. Sayles (1993, Stock #243) $24.95

SPECIAL PACKAGES:
Conversations with CEOs (includes 310 & 316) $16.00
Development & Derailment (includes 136, 138, & 144) $25.00
The Diversity Collection (includes 145, 236, 238, 317, & 320) $85.00
Executive Selection Package (includes 141, 321, & 157) $32.00
Feedback to Managers—Volumes I & II (includes 149 & 150) $85.00
Personal Growth, Taking Charge, and Enhancing Creativity (includes 203, 204, & 205) $20.00
Leadership Education 1996-1997: A Source Book—Volumes 1 & 2 (includes 330 & 331) $60.00

Discounts are available. Please write for a comprehensive Publications catalog. Address your request to: Publication, Center for Creative Leadership, P.O. Box 26300, Greensboro, NC 27438-6300, 910-545-2805, or fax to 910-545-3221. All prices subject to change.

ORDER FORM

Name _____ Title _____

Organization _____

Mailing Address _____
(street address required for mailing)

City/State/Zip _____

Telephone _____ FAX _____
(telephone number required for UPS mailing)

Quantity	Stock No.	Title	Unit Cost	Amount

Subtotal	
Shipping and Handling (add 6% of subtotal with a $4.00 minimum; add 40% on all international shipping)	
NC residents add 6% sales tax; CA residents add 7.75% sales tax; CO residents add 6.2% sales tax	
TOTAL	

METHOD OF PAYMENT

❑ Check or money order enclosed (payable to Center for Creative Leadership).

❑ Purchase Order No. _____ (Must be accompanied by this form.)

❑ Charge my order, plus shipping, to my credit card:
   ❑ American Express   ❑ Discover   ❑ MasterCard   ❑ VISA

ACCOUNT NUMBER:_____ EXPIRATION DATE: MO.____ YR.____

NAME OF ISSUING BANK: _____

SIGNATURE _____

❑ Please put me on your mailing list.
❑ Please send me the Center's quarterly newsletter, *Issues & Observations*.

Publication • Center for Creative Leadership • P.O. Box 26300
Greensboro, NC 27438-6300
910-545-2805 • FAX 910-545-3221

fold here

CENTER FOR CREATIVE LEADERSHIP
PUBLICATION
P.O. Box 26300
Greensboro, NC 27438-6300